My Dear Franchisees

My Dear Franchisees

A day in the life of a franchisor

ANN ANDREWS, CSP

For my dear franchisees who taught me well.

Contents

Part II. My Dear Franchisors

Part III. Franchising Take Two

Reviews

'Having discovered the book *My Dear Franchisees*, it now forms an important part of our introductory material to all new franchisees. I find it an invaluable starting guide for the individual new to the idea of franchising as it is informative, inspiring, re-assuring and humorous. In particular, Section 1, which refers specifically to the relationship that the franchisee and I, as franchisor, will have and the various stages of expectation, frustration and exhilaration that they may experience. The book reiterates a good number of my own personal thoughts and attitudes towards the franchisor/franchisee relationship and presents a clear outline of the prospective franchisee's undertaking and our representative expectations. To date I have only received positive feedback from the book.'

– Karl Sandall, CEO Tax Assist Accountants, Norwich, UK

'I've just finished reading *My Dear Franchisees*. As always invaluable information and expertise. Congratulations and many thanks Ann. I was actually thinking of franchising my own business, but after reading the book, the question now is: 'We can do it (franchise) but is it a good idea?' In other words will the result be up to investment in dollars, time and energy? Thanks for giving me food for thought.'

— Pierre Leonard, CEO, Virtual Words Translations, Belgium

'Ann your book is very impressive and makes great down-to-earth reading. I'm passing my copy on to my GM Franchising Services with a suggestion that it should be compulsory reading for all our new franchisees.'

— Sue Bartlett, Director, Paramount Services, New Zealand

'I've just read your book *My Dear Franchisees* and I want to order a copy for every single one of my franchisees. Every word resonated. I've been trying to tell my franchisees these things for years, now perhaps they will understand. Especially the comment you make that I am NOT their enemy!'

— Warren Mills, Franchisor, SBA Small Business Accounting, New Zealand

'Hi Ann, I've recently read your book *My Dear Franchisees* and absolutely loved it. Read it in about 2 hours. I couldn't put it down.'

— Liz Kanters, Humitech Holdings (NZ) Ltd

Preface

> Decide what you want, what you are willing to exchange for it, and then get going.
>
> — *Helen Hunt*

My first venture into launching my very own business was 'The David Principle Consulting Group Ltd', a human resources/training consultancy specialising in setting up self-managed teams, which, because it was a one-person business (me), involved the dizzy extremes of either too much work or not enough.

One of the challenges for any business, large or small, is to find ways to iron out the financial and physical highs and lows. I still haven't worked out which was worse: having no income and worrying about the bills that were piling up, or having too much work and being constantly exhausted.

On the advice of a coach, my first attempt at ironing out the peaks and troughs was to write a couple of books. This did help a little, but unfortunately, unless you are a Michael Connolly or a J.K. Rowling, books will never make a person rich. So although books gave me credibility in my market, I realised they were not going to smooth out my financial situation to any great degree.

My second attempt at levelling out the time and income dilemma, was to take on trainers.

My rationale was that I could train people in my team process in readiness for winning the really big contracts – something I seemed to be doing at least once a year. Then with one phone call, I could call on these people to assist. A great idea in principle, but the reality was a little different.

If the trainers were any good, they were often too busy themselves and so weren't always available when I needed them. And if they weren't great trainers, I wouldn't want them working with my clients anyway.

So I decided to continue alone and manage the fluctuations as best I could.

Then my partner Warren franchised his business. After a life-long career with the NZ Post Office and subsequently as a senior manager with Telecom, he took voluntary redundancy. He had experienced a few early hiccoughs while trying various ways of earning a living after a lifetime with a government department until the day he set up his own franchise – SBA Small Business Accounting.

I watched with interest.

At first I thought, 'Ah yes, that would work for your kind of business (processing monthly accounts for small businesses) but I don't think it would work for mine (turning whinging, whining groups into high-performing teams).'

Sometimes fate makes decisions for us. I moved into one

of my extremely busy periods again, became incredibly tired and stressed again, and realised I had to do something about my business model before I died of exhaustion.

And so, encouraged by Warren, for the entire year of 2002 I worked on turning part of the work I did with teams into a franchise system. In January 2003 I launched the franchise then known as Teams From Woe To Go (TFWTG), which was basically a six-step process helping business teams deal with never ending change.

I learned so much in those first tortuous years.

Having never been a franchisee, I suspect it can't be an easy life. On the one hand you've bought a business, and yet on the other hand you technically still have a boss (the franchisor) and you still have constraints (the franchise system). So yes, you are your own boss, and yet you still have to answer to someone – and in the early days at least, you most certainly cannot and must not be creative with the system.

Trust me, the life of a franchisor is not an easy one either. After the first few disastrous efforts to recruit franchisees and in sheer frustration one day, I wrote this letter to the rest of my franchisees, trying to get them to understand the hilarious, frustrating, infuriating, rewarding journey we were ALL embarking upon.

I hoped that by highlighting upfront all the things that could and probably would go wrong when people bought into my franchise, if we all occasionally re-read the letter, then hopefully we would be able to flatten out the highs and lows of our franchisee/franchisor relationship.

For you the reader, whether you are a franchisor, franchisee, or a manager, or even a parent, I hope my insights help you realise that the franchisor/franchisee and the manager/employee relationship and the parent/child relationship have a lot of parallels.

They are all challenging relationships.

Enjoy the journey.

'When you come to the end of all the light you know, and it's time to step into the darkness of the unknown, faith is knowing that one of two things shall happen: Either you will be given something solid to stand on or you will be taught to fly.'

−Edward Teller

PART I

IN THE BEGINNING

'The dream begins with a teacher;
someone who pushes you and pokes you with a big
stick called truth.'
– *Goethe*

I.
The letter

My Dear Franchisee,

Know that you are special.

Whether you found me or I found you is irrelevant. The fact that you have become one of my franchisees means that you *are* special, because I am incredibly choosy about the people I want in this business.

In the initial stages of recruiting, I was primarily looking for ex-HR managers, or people with a management background, or even those with a background in training and development. I was wrong. Not that those people aren't unique or special in their own right, or that those skills are not important to what we do – they are very important. But what I realised, after several potential franchisees fell by the wayside, was that I was coming at the recruitment angle from the wrong direction.

I was looking for skills, when I needed to look for some very different attributes. I now have one key criteria and three slightly lesser criteria for selection of my franchisees.

I want to be sure, that whoever joins this business is

passionate about helping other people grow. Part of the way I will teach you to gain business is to run regular showcases and regular workshops. Standing in front of an audience and having them hang on your every word is a heady drug. It is a high to die for. However, it is really easy to stand in front of a group or a conference and get into ego mode: to start believing that you are the oracle. You are not!

There is one promise I can make you, after working with hundreds of teams and presenting just as many showcases and hundreds of workshops – every time you work with an audience, a group or a team, they will teach you as much as you will teach them. Even now after all the years of running my HR business, I'm amazed at how much I still learn every single day. So, if for you, standing in front of a group is about you looking good, then you will fail at this business. People can sniff out ego and arrogance within seconds.

As a professional speaker I was also taught that 5% of my audience will adore me; 5% will most likely hate me, and the rest will fall somewhere in between. The first 5% will give you your buzz, the latter 5% will be your teachers.

Listen well.

The secondary qualities for becoming a franchisee in this business are that:

You must be a self-starter. This is your business and if you don't leap out of bed every morning and hit the road running to talk to clients and sign up business, then any franchise system will fail miserably. You are the business – it's up to you.

You must be coachable. I don't have all the answers (I'm still working on most of the questions!) but because I have been doing this business for a very long time, I do know a lot about what works and what doesn't work. Can you take advice, suggestions, ideas, thoughts, input and feedback from me? Possibly even feedback that you may not like?

You must have tenacity. Like any business, your franchise will take time to establish. It took me seven years to get back to the income I had walked away from as an HR manager in my safe and comfortable job. I promise it will not take you seven years, but it will take time and you must plan for that, financially and emotionally. Because even though you have bought into my system, and even though I know that down the track you will be every bit as good as me (if not better), and even though eventually you will be able to earn a very favourable income, initially you will have to live on very little income.

Potential clients are not buying TFWTG (Teams From Woe to Go), they are buying you, and you will have to establish your own track record and your own client base. You will have to seek out potential clients, and some clients, especially the corporates, take a long time to make a decision.

You will also be up against a lot of competition for the

corporate dollar. There are a lot of good trainers and facilitators out there in the marketplace. You will hear 'no' many times before you hear the wonderful word 'yes'.

Can you stick at this business until it becomes successful?

Do you have what it takes to be in it for the long haul?

Can you take rejection?

Can you re-motivate yourself in your life and in this business when things go wrong?

I believe you have all of the qualities above, but you must believe that too, because I learned very quickly that the secret to selling isn't to be passionate about your product or service, although that is very important.

Ultimately, success in this business is bound up in your ability to sell yourself, and you can't sell yourself if you don't believe in yourself.

Never take no for an answer and never give up. If you really believe in what you're doing and you're really keen, then you'll succeed. It's as simple as that.

—Sir Peter Blake

2.
The question you'll forget I asked you

In one of our very first conversations I would have asked you why you wanted to buy a franchise rather than setting up a business of your own. In my experience, the reasons people have given for wanting to buy into my franchise are:

- I've always wanted to set up my own training business but don't have the capital/know-how/ courage.
- I've been a manager of teams and always enjoyed the team-building aspects of that job.
- I've always wanted to move out of operations (or sales, or HR) and become a full-time team trainer.
- I want to get away from the dreary nine-to-five routine of a job.
- I want to get away from the endless changes of boss I've had over the last few years.
- I want to take charge of my own destiny. I survived the last round of redundancies, but I may not survive the next.
- I'm bored out of my brain with my current profession and want to do something completely different.
- I'm getting to an age where I have outgrown the corporate environment, I'm sick of the politics and the game playing.

- I've gone as far as I can in the corporate world and don't want to spend the next 10–15 years stagnating.

Most people perceive that buying a franchise is a safe way of moving from the world of 'job' and into their own business. And so it is. Statistics show that up to 95% of businesses fail within five years, compared to an almost 90% success rate of franchises.[1]

A franchise is usually a proven system and so won't have the same risks or start-up costs or take quite as long as going it alone in a brand new start-up business. A franchisor will have developed their system over many years and will now be confident that not only does it work, but it is sufficiently refined and simplified that it can easily be taught.

Their belief is that if you follow the system, you will achieve the desired results.

After a while, franchisors will have some established franchisees who have been through those hard times and have built up a successful track record. So if you have just walked away from the world of 'job', you can feel safe

---

1. From *Entrepreneur* magazine: '[Y]ou may land on this gem from About.com: "Some studies show that franchises have a success rate of approximately 90 percent as compared to only about 15 percent for businesses that are started from the ground up. The increased probability of success usually far outweighs any initial franchise fee and nominal royalties that are paid monthly."' – https://www.entrepreneur.com/article/227394

that you have bought a worthwhile business with an in-built safety net. You can also be reassured that you have a support network of other franchisees to call on for moral support if things aren't going so well.

The challenge for me as your franchisor is that because you may have come straight from a job, you will have little or no understanding of what being a business owner entails. You may have little or no experience of:

- Setting up a business for yourself: what that costs and the time it will take.
- The vagaries of income when you're in business (even in a franchise).
- The need for the constant investment of time and dollar in lead generation.
- How to deal with financial planning, and the need to set and stick to a budget. Yes, you may have had a brilliant few months, and yes that red car will really impress potential clients, but how will that affect cash-flow if you have a couple of quiet months down the track?
- How to manage cash-flow over the quiet periods. The days of the monthly salary appearing in your bank account are now over, and December and January are quiet periods in this business. This is great for days at the beach with the family, but not so great if you haven't factored these quiet months into paying your mortgage and feeding your family.
- The need to have a finger on the pulse of cash flow

and credit control, and the skills to deal with slow payers, yet still retain them as future clients. Corporates are notoriously slow payers, some taking as much as 90 days from the date of your invoice to pay you.

- The need to have a strategic plan of your own, not just the one the franchisor has for the business. In other words – where do you want **your** business to be in five years?

We provide a very comprehensive manual: please read it, read it again, and then read it again. Because what is said in any manual, and looks so straightforward on paper, may bear very little resemblance to the actuality of the first few months of being a franchisee.

For example – one of the tasks mentioned in the manual, is that within the first three months of buying your TFWTG franchise, you are asked to contact everyone you know to let them know you are organising your very first showcase.

Have you ever stood in front of a group to make a presentation?

What do you say at the showcase, given that at this stage you will not be familiar with the material we teach?

What if you don't know enough people yet to invite?

How do you advertise, where do you advertise and what if you get no response to those adverts?

Initially I will recommend that you invite people you know. That gives you an opportunity to practice a sales pitch in front of people who care about you and won't mind if you make a few mistakes. This first audience may not be your target market, but they will know people who will know people. That's how showcases work. And who knows, hopefully, even from this very first presentation, you could gain work.

Part of my business and marketing strategy pre-franchising, had always been to speak at business conferences, and one conference I was asked to speak at was for an existing franchise. I confessed that I didn't know much about franchising at that stage, but what the franchisor said has always stuck in my mind. He said, 'Unfortunately people often buy into a franchise for the wrong reasons – some of my franchisees think they've bought a job and act accordingly. They forget that they have actually bought their own business.'

He wanted me to remind them that it's no use sitting behind a counter (it was a retail business) and waiting for customers to come to you, you have to get out there and hustle. In our case, it's no use sitting at home waiting for the phone to ring if you haven't let people know what you are doing and how you can help them.

> 'Sadly my franchisees think they've bought a job'
>
> –Retail franchisor

3.

Being clear what you need from me as your franchisor

I promise you that upon buying your franchise, the learning curve will be immense, particularly if you have never owned your own business before.

At the initial stage, all franchisees will be at the I-don't-even-know-what-I-don't-know stage. A mental state which has been identified as unconscious/incompetence. For example, when we are four years old we don't know that we don't know how to drive a car, but by about eight or nine, we know that we don't know how to drive a car.

If you have never owned your own business, then of course you won't know what owning your own business really means. What you need from me will also depend on your previous work experience.

You may have come from a sales background, so selling will be no problem to you. However marketing may be a challenge for you, and without marketing and letting people know that you have set up your own business, then you have no-one to sell to.

Most franchisees fall into the 80/20 principle:

10% may say, 'I need help with everything!'

If only we had a device that sucked all the knowledge out of a franchisor's head and transferred it into the franchisee's head. Until such a gadget is created, we will have to do this the traditional way. Find a starting point and plan a timetable for the rest.

10% may say, 'I need help with nothing! I don't want you near my business; I am perfectly capable of working this all out for myself.'

These are the scary people for a franchisor! The franchisor knows they don't have a clue about running a business, but the franchisor can hardly say that, and even if the franchisor did say that, they wouldn't hear or understand anyway. When we are in our 'don't-know-we-don't-know' phase, no-one can tell us anything.

These are the two absolute extremes of the franchisee spectrum. You may be one of the 80% of new franchisees who doesn't even know what you need from me, in which case I need you to go away and think about the criteria I set out in chapter three. Rank the challenges in descending order from what you most need help with down to what you feel able to manage for yourself at the moment.

If after doing this exercise you are still not sure how or where to start or feel stressed that you need help with everything on the list, then take a deep breath. Together we will go through your CV to find a logical starting point, and we can put all the rest into some sort of time-line.

> I want pure excitement
> and no risk.
>
> —Unknown

4.
What I need from you as my franchisee

I need you to understand that I am a working franchisor.

I know you probably think I am a multi-millionaire, given that you have just paid me X thousand dollars to join my business. But I am not. I sincerely hope to be one day, but right now I am possibly not much better off than you because I plough virtually every cent that I personally earn, plus everything you pay me, right back into this business so we can all succeed in the long term.

A large part of the franchise fee will go into your initial training. A huge chunk will go into my time to coach and mentor you, because whilst I am training you I am not earning from any other source and I also have business expenses to meet every month. A massive chunk of that initial fee goes into all the things you can't see:

- Maintaining an up-to-date website.
- My initial marketing of you.
- Showing you how the build a database.
- My ongoing marketing of the franchise.
- Administration costs.
- Stationery and other costs.
- The cost of designing and keeping flyers and marketing information up-to-date.
- My time to write a newsletter which you can use,

because writing a newsletter takes time, and while you are doing this you are not doing more important things like networking. This newsletter goes out to all our clients, keeping in touch with them every 30 days or so – by keeping our name in front of them, we stay front of mind and when they have a team challenge they'll call on us rather than a competitor.

I need you to let me know if you need something. I know I look really intelligent; unfortunately my mind-reading gene got lost in the post. If you don't tell me you're stuck, struggling or out of your depth, I won't know and I'll assume you're OK.

I need you to give me time to do things for you. You may decide that you want something. Just pause for a moment and think about what it's likely to cost, and how much time it's likely to take; because what is desirable may not be affordable (yet).

I will do everything within my powers for you, but I have deadlines and budgets of my own, and these will impact on the greater organisation, so I may have to add your requests to my own to-do list. I will, however, give you a time frame as to when I should be able to get back to you.

We are what we repeatedly do.
Excellence, then, is not an act but a habit.

–Aristotle

5.
What you think you've bought and what you've really bought

I know you think you have bought your own business, and to a degree, you have. However, a franchise is slightly different from owning your absolute own business, because what you have actually bought is the right to use a system created by someone else (the franchisor).

I promise you, this will frustrate the hell out of you! Fortunately, you've bought a system that has been tested and proven. I'm not saying it can't be improved; in fact I want every one of my franchisees to be considering ways that we can improve.

However, in the first 12 months of buying into the TFWTG franchise, I need you to follow the system to the letter. Why? Firstly, because it works! Secondly, if you get caught up in trying to change things, it will take your time to do that, which in turn will take you away from sales and marketing, leading very quickly to a lack of income for you. And if you want something changed, I will have to stop what I'm doing to make those changes, and all the manual and workbooks will have to be changed too.

Remember I suggested that you think, 'If I want something, what will it take dollar-wise and time-wise?'

The good news is that every year we will have a conference/get-together. This is the time for us to take things apart and put them back together again!

> The day we think we know everything
>
> Is the day we realise, we know nothing
>
> –Unknown

6.
What you can do with the system, what you can't do with the system

Part of creating a franchise is that immense amounts of time and money have gone into creating letterheads, flyers and other related stationery so that there is a unified 'look' when communicating with potential clients.

I know you probably came up with a really fabulous name for your very own company, and you now want to let people know what that name is.

I want you to think about the fast-food empire of McDonald's, and I then want to ask you – do you think you would be able to purchase a McDonald's outlet and then use your own stationery or marketing logo alongside the McDonald's name and branding? I think not.

And so it is with this franchise. The name is Teams From Woe To Go; that is what you purchased and that is on everything we send out. Sorry! No matter how creative your own company name is, it must not appear anywhere in or on anything to do with this franchise.

You possibly came to the franchise with a background in training and development, or HR, and you may want to sell something other than the TFWTG system to potential clients. Once again – sorry – you absolutely cannot do that without prior consultation with me.

Yet again, think of McDonald's. You would not be able to sell McDonald's food and your own apple pies, no matter how great the apple pies.

The good news is that once you have mastered the six-step process, we can look at adding more products and services to the franchise down-track. And the really great news is that if you have designed that product or service and it is a complementary product we can offer to other TFWTG franchisees, you will be handsomely recompensed for that.

Now isn't that something to aim for?

All I am saying is – be patient. Rome wasn't built in a day or even seven.

> Not getting what you want is sometimes a wonderful stroke of luck.
>
> –The Dalai Lama

7.
What I can do for your business and what I can't

I can give you all the advice in the world; what I can't do is force you to take that advice. If you choose not to take advice, then you must accept responsibility for that.

I can give you all the help in the world in setting up your business, but I can't actually do it for you.

I can help when you make mistakes, but if you don't let me know you are having problems, I can't help. I promise I will not see it as a sign of weakness or failure. I will actually see it as your courage to admit you don't know everything, along with your professionalism in asking before you make a mistake with a client.

In particular, I will see it as your trust in me as your coach and mentor.

I can show you the steps to take to achieve something. What I can't do, if you choose not to follow those steps, is guarantee you will get the desired outcome.

Learn from the mistakes of others; you can't live long enough to make them all yourself.

—Unknown

8.
What I will do for you, what I possibly won't

I take 100% responsibility for the system; I have used it thousands of times and it works.

What I won't do is let you go off on tangents and risk not only your business, but mine and the other franchisees.

And I'm sure that if you think about it, you wouldn't want me to run that risk either. I will support you 100% in creating a successful business. What I won't do is sit back and say nothing if I think you are setting yourself, or TFWTG, up for failure.

Bad planning on your part does not constitute an emergency on my part.

−Unknown

9.

There may be times when I'll say no!

These times will hopefully be rare, but I have to reserve the right to do that.

I may have information or knowledge that you don't have. I have to keep an eye on the big picture at all times.

However I promise if I do say no, I will explain to you why I said no and possibly even discuss other options and/or workable compromises.

I don't want my franchisees to be zombies, but neither can I risk (especially in your first couple of years with me) anyone going off track which may ultimately cause problems for the group as a whole.

No is a complete sentence

−Susan Gregg

10.
What I am, what I'm not

I am your franchisor. I am also your coach and mentor, your cheerleader and your colleague. Your success is my success and vice versa.

However, I am not your mum (or in some cases, perish the thought, your grandmother).

Above all else, I am absolutely not, and never can be, your banker. Please don't leave me at the bottom of your creditor list. If you don't pay me, then I can't pay my creditors, our reputation in the marketplace could be damaged and our business could be put in serious danger.

And the one thing I am not and will never be, is your enemy.

> The Universe is fair and just. We get out of life exactly what we put into it.
>
> –Unknown

II.

What you'll remember I said, and what you'll forget that I said

I promise you that you'll remember me saying, 'You can make a lot of money in this business' however, I can almost guarantee you'll have forgotten that I said, 'It will take 6–12 months to start earning, despite the beautiful forward projections created by an accountant.'

Sadly, life just isn't that simple.

You will remember that I said, 'I'm happy to waive the first year's royalties' you'll forget that I said 'On condition that you get the monthly marketing fees direct credited into my account!'

If I don't receive the marketing fees, there will be no marketing and without regular and constant marketing we will all fade into oblivion.

Success is just a matter of luck. Ask any failure.

—Earl Wilson

12.

The six predictable stages of this journey

Greg Nathan, an Australian psychologist has been both a franchisee and a franchisor, and so he understands the challenges of franchising from both sides of the fence.

In his book *Profitable Partnerships*, he defines six predictable stages you will experience in your first few years.

Stage 1 – Glee

At this stage, you have just purchased your franchise. Hopefully, you will be thrilled, excited, motivated, possibly even ecstatic. You have walked away from a job, freed yourself from those nine-to-five shackles. You are now your own boss. Yeah!

Nathan suggests that this phase can last anywhere from three months to one year, depending on the person, their motivation levels and their previous work history.

Stage 2 – Fee

By now you will have been in business for a while, and the honeymoon period will probably be over.

According to Nathan, by this stage a franchisee has

learned some business realities, such as: Sales minus expenses (especially fees to the franchisor) equals profit. And at this stage there may not be a lot of profit!

My own experience of past franchisees in the fee stage showed their levels of satisfaction dropping exponentially according to effort expended and results being achieved. This is perfectly normal and natural, because at this stage of your franchise, you still don't know what you don't know about the realities of business.

It is at this stage that you will hear yourself asking questions like: 'What am I actually getting for my fees?' 'Why can't I keep this money and do my own advertising/marketing?' 'I'm getting enough work, so why do I need to keep paying money for more marketing and advertising?'

When you realise you are at this stage, I urge you to re-read chapter five and look at the things I'm providing behind the scenes – administration, the website, stationery, and so on; all things you don't have to worry about.

The most important service I provide for you is the website. It took me over six years to build that website, at goodness knows what cost. The master website brings in leads; and if you create your own web-page and link that to the master site, slowly but surely, because of all the activity, we will bring in more and more leads which will convert to work.

Stage 3 – Me

At this stage, Nathan suggests the internal dialogue of any franchisee will probably be: 'I don't need the franchisor ... I can do this myself. My success is due to me; my hard work, my efforts. After all, what does the franchisor actually do? As far as I can see, not a lot. And here I am working my butt off, sending money to him/her – I don't like this set-up at all.'

Nathan describes this as a Self-serving Bias. In other words, when a franchisee is successful they will credit themselves with that success, forgetting all the training, coaching and guidance the franchisor has given them.

The belief at this stage is that the franchisee's success is totally due to themselves. However, Nathan goes on to suggest that if a franchisee is not succeeding, the blame for that is placed fairly and squarely at the feet of the franchisor and/or their useless system!

Nathan warns that at this stage, criticism of the franchisor and/or the system will be high.

Please talk to me if you ever feel you are at this stage.

Stage 4 – Free

If I can't turn your thinking around before you reach the free stage, your frustrations will now be at their highest level and could boil over into a total breakdown in our relationship. It is at this point you'll probably start to think you've made a serious mistake in buying into this franchise.

Nathan suggests that your inner dialogue at this stage will be along the lines of: 'Restrictions, rules, interference: this franchise thing is really holding me back. I know the ropes now, I am successful. I want to do things my way. Why do I have to do everything the franchisor's way?'

This is the ultimate danger zone. Your thoughts of going it alone may become very real.

At this point, I would ask you to seek some wise counsel. Not from lawyers or accountants, or your mum or your dad, or even your best friend's sister who once knew someone who had a franchise that turned to custard.

I don't mean to be disrespectful to any of your friends and relatives, nor do I want to be disrespectful to lawyers and accountants, but by the very nature of their role they will be advising you in isolation from me. Franchising as a business model is still fairly new, and very few lawyers and/or accountants truly understand the business model. Unless they are specialists in franchising, they will miss the point of the place you are at. They will do what accountants and lawyers are paid to do and that is to protect you, their client.

But if they don't truly understand franchising, then the dilemma will be – protect you from whom and protect you from what?

It isn't and never was my intention to rip you off. It was, is and always will be my intention to help you be 100%

successful, because if you are successful then the franchise will be successful.

The franchise relationship is a partnership like any other. If the two parties don't, can't or won't work together to get through this glitch, then parting company can be a very traumatic and expensive option for both of us.

It is normal in this and any franchise contract to have a restriction of trade, so going it alone may not be an option for a considerable period of time I always hope that you feel you can talk to me, but if that isn't an option, I seriously advise you to seek the sage counsel of a long-serving franchisee before you go rushing off to a lawyer.

Chat to someone who has been through all the phases and arrived at a bigger realisation. Because if franchisees are willing to be patient and work through the fee/me/free stages, they then reach a phase Nathan describes as:

Stage 5 – See

And now the inner dialogue becomes: 'Ah, now I see the bigger picture. Now I understand why the marketing is done as a group (leverage). Now I see why the franchisor manages the advertising budget – because if we each managed our own budget, we would probably stop advertising altogether and slowly the work would dry up.

And now I see that there is a reason for branding as a group – because it plants the realisation in the minds of the general public that this is not just a one man/

woman band; this is a country-wide operation and has some serious status.

And now I see why we all have to wear the same uniforms, why our outlets have to look the same, why our phone messages and stationery need to be the same. Ah, and now finally, I see that a franchise is all about...'

Stage 6 – We

'Together we can make this work. Together we can make a difference. Together we have some clout and some power. And if I do my job, and the franchisor does their job, then we help each other along the way and the sky is the limit.

Because finally I see that one of us will never be as strong as all of us!'

We can easily forgive the child who is afraid of the dark. The real tragedy is the adult who is afraid of the light.

–Unknown

13.
My learnings along the way

The first time I advertised my franchise I was swamped with applications from the most amazing people. I ended up taking on seven franchisees and ran a five-day extensive training camp for everyone, teaching them all at the same time.

It seemed like a great idea at the time. Unfortunately, I was in my own 'don't know what I don't know' phase of franchising.

It wasn't a total disaster, but it wasn't far off the mark.

On the fourth day there was a ground swell of disapproval towards one of the participants, so much so that I decided she probably wouldn't work out. If she was causing this much consternation in such a short space of time with my franchisees, what would she be like in front of clients? I decided I couldn't take the risk and so I let her go.

And then there were six.

On the last day of training, a second person decided that a franchise probably wasn't for her. She hadn't realised she would have to get out into the marketplace and sell; she didn't believe she could do that, and no amount of persuasion could allay her fears.

So then there were five.

The third person dropped out after a couple of months when we realised we had different interpretations of what she had bought and what I had actually sold. I now realise I probably didn't receive the best legal advice: I had been very clear I was selling franchises, yet the contract clearly talked about 'the license'. This person believed categorically that she had bought a license and was at liberty to tack my products onto her own, take my name off everything, put her name on everything and even change all my branding to her branding!

I gave this person a 100% refund of her fees.

Now there were four.

The fourth and fifth people to drop out were a couple. One was really passionate about the business but the other wasn't. Sadly, the person who had all the passion would have been working behind the scenes on the administration side of their business, while the person who was ho hum would've been the up-front trainer! Not a good look.

Then there were two.

Another of my awesome people had a marriage break-up!

Now there was one.

And my final person decided she actually wanted to go it alone with her own products.

So finally there were none.

A 100% clear-out in less than 12 months!

At this stage I was ready to walk away from the whole franchise thing. It was just too hard. On the face of it, these were my *dear* franchisees – the ones that had cost me dearly in time, emotion and money.

However, I had to take responsibility for the 100% turnover. To be totally honest, this was a brand new business model for me; I didn't really know what I was doing, I certainly didn't really know the types of people I was looking for, and I absolutely didn't know what the pitfalls were likely to be in the early stages for any of us.

Fortunately, I went to a franchise meeting and sought some sage counsel myself. I was advised that every franchise goes through this turmoil in the first year. Statistics even suggest that a virtual 100% turnover in the first year isn't unusual. Phew.

It restored my faith in me, and it restored my faith in my system.

'What doesn't kill you will make you stronger'

−My Grandmother

14.
understanding 'The Life of Brian'

During one of my 'what-the-heck-was-I-thinking?' phases, I watched the Monty Python movie 'The Life of Brian' for the zillionth time.

The 'what-have-the Romans-ever-done-for-us' sketch leapt out at me as being the perfect story to explain the franchisee/franchisor relationship.

When I wrote the chapter and showed it to my partner, he asked if I realised that Greg Nathan had also alluded to the very same scene in his book *Profitable Partnerships*. I was absolutely devasted, because although I had seen a graph of the six emotional stages of a franchisee, I had never actually read Nathan's book (sorry Greg).

So what to do?

I didn't want to appear to be plagiarising and yet, no matter how much I wracked my brains, I just couldn't come up with any other story or analogy which fitted so well to explain this challenging alliance.

So I tracked down his book and read his reference to the movie. Having read it, I realised that I had planned to write the scene in full, whereas he has only made a very small reference to it, so I felt comfortable using the scene.

So here it is.

In the particular scene from 'The Life of Brian', John Cleese, in his role as the leader of the People's Front of Judea (not the Judean People's Front) was trying to incite his followers to revolt against the occupying Romans.

He asked the hypothetical question, 'What have the Romans ever done for us?' A little voice piped up from the background. 'The aqueducts?' To which Cleese responds, 'Alright, but apart from the aqueducts, what have the Romans ever given us?'

Another little voice suggests, 'Sanitation?' Cleese replies, 'Agreed, they gave us sanitation. But apart from the aqueducts and sanitation, what have the Romans ever done for us?'

'Roads?' another revolutionary suggests. 'I admit, they've given us the aqueducts, sanitation and roads, but apart from that what have they ever done for us?'

'Mmmmm – education ... wine ... medicine ... irrigation ... fresh water ... public health?' come replies from various parts of the room. In a final burst of frustration, Cleese agrees. 'All right, but apart from the sanitation, medicine, education, wine, public order, irrigation, roads, a fresh water system, and public health – what have the Romans ever given us?'

'Peace?' another voice quietly suggests.

I use this hilarious sketch to illustrate that there will be many, many times when you as a franchisee will ask the question: 'What has the franchisor ever done for me?'

When you do ask this question, please remember John Cleese and the People's Front of Judea – because just like the Romans, whether you like your franchisor or not, he/she has set up the business into which you bought. He/she took the risks, wrote the manuals, tested the process, built the website and invested in marketing and sales.

'The truth will set you free but first it will irritate the heck out of you'

–A mangled version of John 8:31-32

15.

The dream is bigger than both of us

So, my dear franchisee, whatever else you forget, never forget that I said I support you 100%.

Never forget I said I will be with you every step of the way, not just in the first month or the first year, but for as long as you need me.

And never forget that you are, indeed, a very special person.

I now recruit only the very best for this business and I would not have recruited you if I didn't think you've got what it takes to make a success of your franchise.

Welcome to the dream.

Welcome to the adventure.

When you believe in someone you profoundly increase their ability to have faith in themselves and achieve.

—Jason Versey, A *Walk with Prudence*

PART II

MY DEAR FRANCHISORS

'A coach's role is to tell people what they'd rather not hear, let them see what they'd rather not see so they can become who they are capable of being.'
— *Unknown*

16.
understanding leadership

Anyone who ever said that being a leader was easy has probably never actually been a leader.

The franchisor of a business is quite naturally the leader of the business, and therein could lie a problem if the franchisor isn't a natural leader.

Leadership requires courage; a clear vision and a solid set of values by which the parameters of the business will run. Great leaders don't work from ego; they have no fear of surrounding themselves with people who are smarter than them. I've always viewed leadership as a 'strategic' skill and management as a more 'operational' talent.

There are even different types of leader.

Autocratic leaders tend to want to make all the decisions; are usually reluctant to hand over power to anyone and firmly believe that no-one is as smart as they are. The extremely autocratic leader leans towards being a bully.

Democratic leaders tend to be more open and inclusive. They are happy to share power and encourage input on idea generation and decision making.

Laissez faire leaders are more 'hands-off'. They tend to have a closed door policy leaving people to work things out for themselves. This is a leadership style which can lead to poor decision making and low productivity.

I firmly believe that a great leader is a mix of all three of these styles; it is what I call 'know when to hold 'em and know when to fold 'em'. In other words, know when to step in and take control of a situation, yet know when to stand back and allow people to make decisions themselves.

There are numerous sub-sets of leadership styles – some are the natural personality of the leader in question, others are more to do with the situation the leader is facing at the time.

The charismatic leader is a person who has an abundance of charm and personality. These leaders naturally attracts people with his or her sheer passion and personality. This could be a democratic leader with personality, and even an autocratic leader with a touch of pizzazz. Think ex-President Clinton, ex-President Obama and Richard Branson.

The visionary leader: someone who has a clear picture in mind of what the future looks like and can paint that picture so others will be inspired by it and join him or her on the journey. Think Gandhi or Kennedy.

The strategic leader: a person with the skills required in a start-up or new team. Someone who has the big picture clearly in mind and will take a new team or group along with him or her confidently during the early stages of a business. These people don't necessarily court the limelight. Think Bill Gates.

The transitional leader: required when a business has sudden growth or takes over another business. A person who has a steady hand and doesn't panic easily. A person who has the long game in mind; someone who can hold everything together during a traumatic period. Theresa May tried to be this person after the UK public voted to leave the EU. Sadly and for a variety of reasons, she failed the task.

The situational/facilitative leader: someone who can coordinate the people, processes and skills required at a particular time in the life cycle of a business. Someone who can bring those different factions together and help them find a way through to consensus and a desired outcome. Think Sir Winston Churchill who took over as prime minister of the UK after the outbreak of the Second World War.

The operational leader: someone who can literally step in, become hands on if need be to get things happening, get things moving. He or she can clearly see the challenges and can implement systems to smooth out operational road blocks.

Management is a very different talent.

A good manager will take the company's vision and turn it into workable systems and processes. Some leaders can manage, some managers can lead, but neither switch is guaranteed or in some cases is it even a natural switch.

Should a franchisor be a leader or a manager?

Initially a franchisor has to be everything to everybody, but given time, and a healthy ego, a good franchisor will realise he/she can't be everything to everybody and will very quickly bring in the people who have the skills they don't have.

Some of us don't know what to do without people and papers to push around; others don't know what to do without people to push them around.

−Charles Handy

17.
utilising the staggering power of profiling

Let me say up front that there are dozens if not hundreds of profiling tools on the market. Hippocrates is credited with being the first person to realise that although every single person is unique, there are similarities in certain 'types' of people.

I'm about to share with you 4 different profiling tools. All are relevant at some stage of your franchise.

As a franchisor your style of being and doing will form the basis of everything about your business. If things are working well, all hail you, if things are not working well, you will need to acknowledge that everything good and bad stems from you also.

At some stage, every franchisor needs to have the courage to bring in whatever help is needed to take the business to the next level. Tough to hear I know. I've already said that different situations require different leadership styles; what works at one point could be dangerous at another stage of growth.

Because I came from an HR background and had worked with teams for so many years before I set up my franchise, I understood the different personality types well. I've always urged owners, managers and team leaders to be profiled themselves, and to profile anyone they are about to recruit or promote.

Profiles won't tell you everything about the person, you still need to do background checks and check references, but they give you a pretty fair idea of the 'personality' of the person and the behaviours that go along with their personality.

This is another of those 'buts' I hear regularly. 'Ah yes but they are pretty expensive.' Some are, some are free, however, the cost of employing the wrong person or promoting the wrong person is infinitely more costly than not investing in a profile.

Understanding a person's personality type will also help you coach and mentor them to give of their best.

I've interviewed hundreds of people in my years as a personnel and human resources manager and sadly, in the early days of my career, made quite a lot of recruitment and even promotion mistakes. Initially in the interview process, I took people at face value and trusted that what they were telling me was the truth. I believed every word they said when they answered my carefully prepared interview questions. It was only much later in my interviewing career that I realised people were often telling me what they thought I wanted to hear.

Why?

Maybe they were desperate for a job; perhaps they were just sick of going along to interviews that led nowhere and so were willing to say anything and agree to anything, to get whatever job I was interviewing them for.

The tragedy of employing the wrong person is that it is a lose-lose situation. It doesn't work for the organisation or business because they now have a person who isn't right for the job you are offering (or franchise you are selling) and it doesn't even work for the person you've employed because within a very short space of time they will realise they are out of their depth or in the wrong job and they too will be miserable.

Whatever the rationale of people telling me what they thought I wanted to hear, I decided I had to get better at this recruiting thing. The employment contract is a bit like a marriage: easy to get into, but very time-consuming and costly to get out of.

And then I heard about a process for 'profiling' candidates, often referred to as psychometric testing.

Profiling tool number 1: The four temperaments

Hippocrates identified what he called the four temperaments. His aim was to better understand the health issues of each temperament and his classifications are still used by many traditional practitioners of medicine around the world today.

The four temperaments he identified were:

Choleric (relates to yellow bile). He noticed that these people were goal orientated, analytical and logical. Not necessarily social beings, they dislike small talk, preferring to be with people who have similar professional and intellectual interests. These people can tend to be intolerant, overpowering, poor listeners and dismissive of other people's ideas.

Melancholic (relates to black bile). These were people he noticed who liked tradition, who do not look for novelty or adventure. They are orderly, love detail and need accuracy. They also work best with clearly defined laws, rules and regulations. The downside of this temperament is that they are incredibly risk averse, need way too much information before they make a decision and wait far too long to abandon outdated systems. They become very stuck in habitual ways.

Phlegmatic (relates to phlegm). These people he realised were all about relationships. They do not like conflict and will always try to mediate so that harmony and peace are restored between family members, friends and even neighbours. Their downside is that they get side-tracked into other people's problems and tend to lose sight of their own challenges and deadlines.

Sanguine (relates to blood). The sanguine personality is a very social person. They love to be with people. They are outgoing, handshaking, touching people. They bring life and energy into a room by their very presence. The downside is that they can exhaust others with their energy and desire for never ending change. They can also be very loud people.

Even to this day, some 30 years after I was first introduced to the concept of profiling, I find still find there is resistance. People fear being put in a 'box' when in fact profiles don't do that. We are all a mix of the temperaments and styles and behaviours. We all have our dominant traits and our least traits which simply translate into our strengths and weaknesses.

No-one is perfect.

No-one.

No-one can be everything to everybody.

No-one.

Over the years since Hippocrates first identified these four temperaments, there have been hundreds of variations on that basic profiling/psychometric testing theme. I trialled what is known as the 'bird' profiling tool when I first started working with teams. It always felt less threatening to people and even ended up being lots of fun for people who had never been exposed to such a science before.

Profiling tool number 2: The 'bird' personalities

An Owl personality = the Melancholic

A Dove personality = the Phlegmatic

A Hawk personality = the Choleric

A Peacock personality = the Sanguine

Sales people are traditionally seen as peacocks; HR people tend to be predominantly doves; and our accounting people tend to be our owls. You will frequently hear the term 'hawk' with regard to leaders and managers. Hawks are the Autocratic leaders and can be tough bosses; people who appear to care only about the bottom line. In politics, Hawks are viewed as the warmongers.

Even profiling isn't the be all and end all; it will only ever be part of a recruitment process. References still need to be checked and it always pays to have more than one person interview a prospective candidate to offer their perceptions of a candidate.

A rule of thumb in recruiting is to beware of recruiting in our own image. We like people like us, and so we end up with sales teams full of peacocks and accounts departments full of owls. The problem with that is that they all think the same. Teams actually need all four personalities so that problems are solved using all the talents and viewing a problem from all angles.

For example, during a problem-solving exercise, Owls are likely to ask, 'How much will this cost and what are the rules for implementation?' Doves will almost certainly ask, 'Who will this decision affect?' Peacocks could quite probably ask, 'Is there a bonus structure around this?' And the Hawks will absolutely want to know, 'When will this be done?'

The beauty of using profiles in a recruitment and even promotion phase is that they show up any anomalies from what the person says at interview are their talents, and what the profile 'shows' their natural talents to be. A profile may also confirm that the person is answering questions in a way that you were thinking 'this doesn't feel right'.

If I'm looking for a salesperson (Peacock) and at the interview the person assures me that they have great sales skills yet the profile of the person clearly shows that this person is actually a deeply analytical personality (Owl), then sales skills are not likely to be one of their talents. I then know that the person is telling me what I want to hear, which is a recipe for disaster for both of us.

Why can't people be more like me

–Unknown

18.
A very simple franchisee profiling concept

Every franchisor should read the book *The E Myth* before they even think of recruiting their first franchisee. Michael Gerber talks about three 'working styles' and is clear that we all have two of the styles, but no-one has all three.

Profiling tool number 3: the 'working styles'

Technicians. These people like doing the doing. If you are launching a 'hair styling' franchise, they will love doing 'hair'. If you are launching an accounting franchise, they will love beavering away doing accounts. These are our front end people, the loyal people who happily beaver away for us. The problem here will be if you want them to grow their business; they are not hugely interested in stepping back and taking on a more managerial role.

Managers. These people are really great at creating and improving systems. And given a franchise is a 'system' having one of these as a franchisee can be a blessing or a nightmare (see Chapter 6 – What you can do, what you can't do). Eventually once they really understand your business then absolutely get them involved in improving your system, just not in their early days. The danger is that they will drive you insane wanting to change everything, now, today, this minute.

Entrepreneurs. These are the 'ideas' people; the high energy ones who will fall passionately in love with your concept. The downside is that once they have quickly learned the ropes (and they learn very quickly), they will be bored with the restrictions you have imposed and will probably set off in business in direct competition to you using all the things you have taught them, even your very precious system.

Ideally you will be looking for a 'technician' with a touch of 'manager' or preferably a 'manager' with a touch of 'technician' because in the early days your franchisee will have to be everything to everybody, until they can afford to bring on board their first staff members. THEN they will be able to step back from doing the doing and become more of a manager; helping their staff to achieve results rather than being the person who has to do that themselves.

Train people well enough so they can leave. Treat them well enough so they don't want to.

−Sir Richard Branson

19.
How to bring out the very best in your franchisees

There will always be franchisees we will get on with better than others. There will be franchisees who work harder than others – and these may not even be the ones that you like. And for sure there will be slackers; deniers; blamers and franchisees who out and out annoy the heck out of you.

It's the old adage: 80% of your people will just get on with the things you've taught them, and the remaining 20% will take up 80% of your time and energy and give you the most grief. So for your sanity's sake you have to find a way to work with them so they don't give you sleepless nights.

When working with teams I've always told them that they don't have to 'like' the people they work with, which invariably surprises them. What I suggest they do is let go of the need to 'like' their co-workers and to take some time to discover their particular skills and talents, and to respect them for those. Strangely enough, when we let go of the need to 'like' a person and take the time to 'respect' them, a strange thing happens, we then end up 'liking' those people.

It's exactly the same with your franchisees – you don't

have to 'like' them. However, it is vital that you take time to understand their skills and talents so you can bring out the very best in them. Liking them is simply not important.

So how do you get past actually not liking someone, to then spend time discovering their skills and talents?

You 'man up' (or woman up) and take time to get to know them. Abe Lincoln once said, 'I don't like that man. I must get to know him better'. And so it is with your franchisees. They've invested in you so you now need to invest in them. And you do that by having regular one-to-ones with them. Particularly in the early days. Talk to them, find out about their families; find out about their interests and hobbies. Find some common denominators.

Time spent building strong relationships with your people, whether you like them or not, is never wasted. If you establish a good rapport from day one, this will save you hours and hours of stress and pain in the later months if you then find you have to reign them in on something they are doing. Having regular one on ones with your franchisees is vital. The worst thing a franchisor can do is let a relationship with a franchisee deteriorate to a point where you can't bear to be in each other's company.

In my book *Did I Really Employ You?* I quote a statistic which says that in the case of an employee, it can cost anything from between two and a half times a person's salary to 24 times their salary to replace them. I would imagine the cost of poor franchise recruitment will reflect the same huge costs.

These costs are incurred not just because of placing endless advertisements, nor in the time it takes to go through the protracted interview process; rather because of the wasted training, wasted management time trying to improve performance, mistakes made during the training process, damage they can do to customer relationships, and the clients or information they may steal when they leave.

In order to better understand this whole 'franchising' thing for myself, I attended a Global Franchising Summit in Auckland in 2005. Delegates at the summit were from Japan, China, Malaysia, Australia, Singapore and New Zealand.

What was fascinating was that everyone who spoke at the conference acknowledged they had the same problems – finding good people and holding onto them.

In the early days of franchising, most of the franchisors agreed they'd initially thought that if a person could afford the entry fee they could buy a franchise. They had all come to the realisation that this is really short-term thinking, and most have revised their recruitment practices to recruiting people with a great attitude, even if it means selling their franchises more slowly or arranging payment on an instalment plan.

So in this looking-for-an-awesome-franchisee process, if

there was anything that could help me not have a 100% clear-out ever again, I wanted to know about it.

It is equally important that a potential franchisee also knows whether they have what it takes to be a franchisee. They are going to invest their hopes and dreams with you, not to mention their own life savings.

If they don't have the right skills and talents, it's best that they know at the start. Yes they will be disappointed, but isn't it better for them to know they don't have the right skill-set than to end up being bitter and twisted after a failed franchise and losing their substantial investment?

> Sure I'd love to see your cousin's roommate's dentist's daughter's resume
>
> —Not known

FRANCHISING TAKE TWO

It's as important to figure out what you're not going to do as it is to know what you are going to do.

– *Michael Dell*

20.
When the going gets tough (and at some stage in every business the going WILL get tough)

Whatever business we have launched, it's really important to look after yourself during the highs and lows.

It's OK to take time out every now and again to go and play golf; go fishing; play tennis or even head out for a swim. Our bodies need a break from our over-active brains occasionally. When we give ourselves permission to take a day off or to have a massage, strange things happen. It's as if our brains go into a different mode. We may start to reflect or reconsider. We may get an idea that helps us through whatever block we are facing.

Working harder and harder, and longer and longer hours actually solves nothing and can lead to burn-out, health problems and even mental or physical break downs.

Pace yourself.

Something I've always loved doing is getting together with a group of like-minded and probably equally exhausted business owners, either informally for breakfast to share our troubles and gripes. or more formally in the form of starting or belonging to a Mastermind group (see the appendix for how to start one).

Often others in our group have faced whatever challenge we are dealing with and can offer tips. Or we can sit back while others brainstorm ideas for us – some may not work but one or two could be just the breakthrough you need.

Over the years I've worked with thousands of business owners and one of the things I've always tried to get them to do is to take one afternoon off per week and to get right away from business.

I'm always met with what I call – the 'buts'.

'Ah yes, but then what would happen if a decision has to be made and I'm not there?'

Solution: leave one of your senior people in charge and give them permission to make decisions – clearly you will have to decide which decisions they can't make but if you never learn to delegate then you'll probably drop dead at the wheel.

My next suggestion with owners is to 'get help'. And the 'but' here will be:

'That sounds good in principle, but right now I can't afford to do that.'

To which I reply, 'If you want to grow your business, then you actually can't afford NOT to get help'.

I recently worked with a young business owner who was literally so stressed that he spent the days yelling at everyone in his team, and his nights walking along the beach because he couldn't unwind enough to sleep. That is actually a stage of stress called 'overwhelm' – and it's an incredibly dangerous place to be.

I knew that unless this young man made some decisions about getting help, I actually feared for his life. We know that we have a worldwide suicide problem, particularly with young men. Asking for help seems to be really hard for them to do.

He ran a small building company and first thing in the mornings seemed to be manic. Perhaps a worker hadn't shown up or someone was stuck on the motorway. Perhaps a supplier had let them down at the last minute and irate customers were on the line. All challenges for any building company I would predict. So every morning this was his reality, stress, frustration, anger and confusion, five days a week. His day was then spent catching up on paperwork, complaints, rework, rescheduling of jobs, trying to find urgent supplies.

I suggested bringing in someone five mornings a week simply to take phone calls; to prioritise the urgent ones and to hand them to him just after lunch. That way his mornings were not beset by endless interruptions. I suggested also that he decide which of his staff he felt was suitable to promote to team leader, so THEY could deal with the staffing problems, and he could deal with supply and customer issues. I wanted him to schedule his week going forward so that he took Friday afternoons off, being a building company, by Friday lunch time most of their jobs were either in progress or finished or were being re-scheduled to the following week.

He took every bit of advice on board and made changes that probably saved his life.

And a few things were about to massively change my life.

Again.

We all understand the importance of asking for help, those who achieve big things are the ones who accept it when it is offered.

−Simon Sinek

21.
When the going gets tough, the tough keep going

Off I went again with recruitment and I found three truly amazing people.

Off I went with their training. I ran various breakfast events to introduce them to my client base. I ran workshops with them and for them until they were able to take over running them without me.

And all three were amazing.

Then life hit.

My mother had been diagnosed with a particular form of cancer seven years previously. With the drug regime she was placed on, she had managed to live a reasonably normal life, however she had been warned that 5–7 years was probably about as long as the drugs would keep her alive.

In February, 2005 I got the dreaded call that I needed to go home. I live in New Zealand, my mother lived in the UK. So home I went, fearing the worst.

I spoke to my franchisees and they understood that I had to go. By this stage all three were totally able to stand alone. They had all proved that they absolutely could make their franchises work. So safe in that knowledge, I went back to the UK to be with my mum.

Imagine my complete surprise then, when I rushed into the hospital and found her sitting in an armchair, fully dressed and waiting to be discharged. She was so tiny and frail that I couldn't believe they were even considering sending her home to look after herself. But my mum was a determined woman – she wanted to go home, and home she was going.

So I got to take my mum home and look after her for three very precious weeks. All too fast the day came when I had to leave to return to New Zealand. Walking out and leaving her was the hardest thing I've ever done. I knew she was in safe hands with my family, but I also knew my mum didn't have much longer to live and so I would have given anything to stay. But I had a business to run and franchisees who depended on me.

My mum realised very quickly that she couldn't cope alone any longer and so finally asked to go into a hospice. Around the middle of April I got the final call. And so, barely seven weeks after I got back to New Zealand I was back on a plane again, this time absolutely convinced that I wouldn't get back in time. But I did. I managed to be with my mum for her last four days. She slipped away peacefully in her sleep on the 26th April, 2005.

Meanwhile, my franchise had fallen apart. Again.

One of my amazing people had realised that he simply

didn't have the network to keep going. He had two small children and his lack of income was putting a serious strain on his family, and so he asked to be released from his contract to take a job he had been offered. He left with my absolute blessing.

A second franchisee had secured some great team opportunities with a company who asked him to become their in-house trainer. I discussed this with him, warning him that in a recession, the first person to get the chop is either the company trainer or the company HR person. But ditto − I said, if this is what he wanted I absolutely wouldn't stand in his way. He chose to take the job. Sadly about 18 months later he was made redundant.

And then there was one.

After my mum died and I got back to NZ I realised that I hadn't seen any reports for a while from my one remaining franchisee, yet before I left on the final trip home I had passed a very substantial contract over to her. Once I got my land legs back I called her to see how she was and to check on the team I had left her with. She informed me that the company had decided not to go ahead, hence not putting in a report because she hadn't had any work.

By strange coincidence, this client called me to let me know how happy he was with the way she was performing! So my second call was rather unpleasant. She accused me of checking up on her; I let her know that the client had called me.

My fees were 5% of any work I passed on. I had passed on a contract for $28,000, so for a measly $1400 dollars she had tried to cheat me during a time when I was burying my mother.

I closed her down that very day.

And then there were none.

Again.

So what had I not learned?

How come I was right back where I had been a couple of years before?

Had I chosen the wrong business model?

Should I have licensed the business rather than franchising it?

The easiest way out usually leads back in

−Peter Senge

22.
Am I the problem?

So I was now two attempts down.

Even though Warren (now my husband) tried everything he knew to persuade me not to give up, I just knew that emotionally I wasn't ready to try advertising for franchisees again. I hadn't totally given up but I needed to grieve for my mum; I needed to work on my own again for a while, and I needed time to think through my 'what next'.

And as always – when the student is ready a teacher appears.

Because I was so passionate about profiling, I had become a trained 'profiler' myself. I'd now taken all manner of profiling tests myself and administered them for literally thousands of people, but the profiles I had encountered were all to do with behaviours. So when I heard that an 'Entrepreneurial' profiler was coming to town, I signed up for his session.

Profiling tool number 4: 'Wealth Dynamics' profiling

Roger Hamilton built on the traditional Hippocrates model and created a 'Wealth Dynamics' profiling tool; a way to discover how various people make their money, and the most suitable businesses for each entrepreneurial style to enter into. He defined these styles as:

The Mechanic. A person who builds and creates systems. Think Henry Ford, Ray Kroc, Sam Walton, Michael Dell. ('Mechanic' is a perfect style for a franchisor.)

The Lord. This person controls the cash that generates the assets. Think Andrew Carnegie, John D Rockefeller, John Paul Getty.

The Accumulator. A person who collects accumulating assets. Think Benjamin Graham, Warren Buffet, Paul Allen.

The Trader. This entrepreneur buys low and sells high. Think George Soros, Peter Lynch, John Templeton, Jim Rogers.

The Deal Maker. A deal maker brings people together. Think Rupert Murdoch, Donald Trump (though perhaps this has now been proved NOT to be his style) and David Geffen.

The Supporter. A person who leads the team. Think Jack Welch, Michael Eisner, Steve Case.

The Star. This person creates a unique brand that is about them. Think Oprah Winfrey, Martha Stewart, Arnold Schwarzenegger, Paul Newman. I believe this is where Trump should be – he is the ultimate showman!

The Creator. Invents and/or creates a better product. These entrepreneurs are people like Thomas Edison, Walt Disney, Bill Gates, Steve Jobs, Richard Branson.

If you've ever experienced light bulbs going off all around

you, that is what hit me sitting in that workshop. I was trying to build a Mechanic business when in my heart and soul I realised I am a Creator/Supporter. No wonder my heart wasn't in it.

I knew then that I couldn't keep the franchise going. YES, I could have recruited again, after all I'd proved that the system worked. But I'd found no joy in the business model itself, even though I loved helping the various franchisees get going. The whole point of the franchise had been to hand over my 'system' and earn a passive income from it. I was not, and never would be, a 'Mechanic'. It didn't fill my soul.

I finally decided that it was time to close my franchise for good.

> Many times what we perceive as an error or failure is actually a gift. And eventually we find that lessons learned from that discouraging experience prove to be of great worth.
>
> —Richelle E Goodrich

23.
Out of the ashes

A lovely friend of mine, a fellow speaker and author taught me to ask these three questions if I felt my business was stagnating:

What have you got?

What else could you do with it?

Who else could be interested?

What I was left with was 30 years' worth of knowledge about all things HR. I had a clear understanding from speaking at so many events, that every business needed that knowledge and I had an absolute desire to hand my knowledge and experience over to the people that needed it and wanted it. Just not in the form of a franchise.

Within weeks I had launched an online training company.

Over the next seven years I built a database of 15,000 customers; I represented 400+ authors, speakers, trainers and coaches and I sold THEIR books and training programmes on-line, from the comfort of my office, most days wearing my fluffy slippers.

In 2017 I received an offer for the business I couldn't refuse.

So I didn't.

> We are continuously faced with great opportunities disguised as insoluble problems
>
> –Unknown

24.
There really are no mistakes

The first version of this book was written out of my own frustration that day when my then franchisees just didn't 'get' how hard I was working for them and I was feeling very sorry for myself.

Warren, my husband, a franchisor of some 32 retail accounting outlets, read the letter and said, 'I want a copy for all my franchisees'. Which surprised me – he was so much further along the journey than me, yet he was still having tear-your-hair-out days.

So as I was putting the finishing touches to this updated version, I asked him what he would do differently with his franchise if he was to start again.

Having built SBA Small Business Accounting to 32 franchises throughout New Zealand and Australia, which to all intents and purposes was a successful franchise, his problem was the massive toll it was taking on his health.

Warren absolutely falls into the 'Mechanic' profile and so, on paper, was the perfect person to set up a franchise business. After leaving his job as a manager in the New Zealand Post Office, where he was famous for being able to go into an outlet and literally sort out their systems, he set up his own small accounting business working for what he called 'shoe box' businesses, those one person businesses who at the end of each financial year would arrive on his doorstep literally with their shoe box full of receipts, having no idea how to reconcile their business profits or losses.

He had seen an opportunity to give these businesses a monthly service, so every month they knew exactly where their cash flow was rather than waiting a year or even 18 months to find out whether they were running a profitable business or not which was how traditional accountants worked in those days.

Warren's point of difference when he built the franchise was that his outlets were street level on busy thoroughfares (not up some back stairs as most accountant's offices are) so they were very visible to passing traffic.

The upside for Warren was that he is a 'Mechanic' profile; the downside is that he is a 'Mechanic' profile. Warren is also a 'technician/manager', so put all that together and what he fully acknowledges he was NOT good at, was dealing directly with the franchisees. Warren is not great with people issues and he absolutely hates conflict.

We had a chuckle one afternoon as he reflected on his 'worst' franchisee experiences.

He had one person who felt she was perfectly entitled to bring her very large dog into her office. Not everyone likes dogs, and eventually anywhere you have a dog you will have a dog smell. He spent several weeks of frustration trying to explain to her that he did not want her dog in the office; that it wasn't professional and that he had had complaints from a few customers who actually found the dog intimidating.

Another franchisee – also on a street front position on a busy street, insisted on keeping the shop lights off and his door closed. And so of course, it looked as if his operation was 'closed'. Once again Warren explained that he had to keep lights on so people knew he was open for business. The franchisee's explanation was that he couldn't afford to keep the lights on because he wasn't attracting many customers. A classic circular argument.

Warren realised that his biggest mistake was in not recognising that he needed to bring in an operations manager or even and HR manager once these 'people' challenges started happening. He needed someone who could build those relationships with his franchisees; someone who could handle the people/performance/ professionalism issues in a way that he knew he couldn't.

In the end Warren also had someone express an interest in buying his business and so after a couple of years of serious health issues, brought on by the stress of managing 32 franchise outlets, he realised that he simply had to get out.

Each man should frame life so that at some future hour, fact and his dreaming meet.

—Victor Hugo

25.
In the final analysis

This book was originally written for franchisors but I also urge anyone in business to read this book. Managers get just as frustrated with employees and employees get just as ticked off with their managers.

Here's a thought for franchisees also.

As franchisees start to grow their franchise and find they need to take on staff, they will realise that all the things I've said here for franchisors, owners and managers, are the very things they will be saying, doing and feeling when they need to recruit and manage staff. Some will be a joy and others will make them want to tear their hair out!

I also urge anyone in business to invest in a profile for themselves, so they know exactly what their strengths are, but also where their weaknesses lie. The number one skill in being a leader is knowing how and where **you** are causing problems.

The single biggest leap forward for anyone in business, is when leaders know exactly the skills and talents they don't possess and are willing to recruit people with the skills they lack to fill the gaps.

Profiling needs to become a standard part of how people

do business. Understanding what makes people tick will save everyone's sanity. I promise.

NB: You will find a link for a free profile at the end of this book.

Appendix: How to Set Up a Mastermind Group

I was very fortunate in my early days as a would-be speaker to be invited to be part of a MASTERMIND group. I'm absolutely convinced that it's because of those wonderful people who encouraged, coaxed, counselled and pushed me, that my business became as successful as it did.

We were also very fortunate that our group lasted several years, but I have heard that many groups simply don't last. Perhaps members join for the wrong reason, or lose faith during the process, which is a shame, because if they really stuck to the group meetings (and yes I know people say they are too busy) then it would become something that they simply would never miss.

A MASTERMIND group is really an appointment with yourself. It's that working ON your business, not IN it. So if you are thinking of setting up a MASTERMIND group, these tips and thoughts could be of value.

What exactly is a MASTERMIND group?

It's a group of like-minded people who want to support

each other in taking the next giant leap in their business thinking and results. The ideal number of people in the group is seven, however any number up to eight is OK; more than that and the dynamics can become too cumbersome.

Before you start, think very carefully about who you would like to have in your group:

- Positive people are a must – negative people drain the group's energy
- Choose people who are entrepreneurial (willing to take a few risks)
- Choose people who want to look for 'solutions' rather than a place to dump their 'problems'
- Choose people who are self- starters, not people who want to use the group to PUSH them along. Too tiring.

Before you start the group

Each person will need to take time to do some personal work:

WHERE? Each person has to think about their ultimate vision or goal. Where are they going? What is their desired finishing post? When setting this goal it is always advisable to remember the balance of home, work and actually having a life.

WHY? Each person needs to think long and hard about why this vision or goal is important to them. Often once we explore the why we may realise that we are doing things for all the wrong reasons. Like 'I want to be stinking rich.' Why? 'So that I can skite to all those people who didn't think I would amount to anything!'

HOW? What roles will you play in order to achieve your Vision? (e.g. writer/speaker/trainer/consultant). We are all multi-faceted but no-one can be all things to all people. Some aspects of what we currently do will take us towards that vision, other things we are doing could take us away. When setting off in business the greatest mistake we make is to try to be everything to everybody so some hard choices may have to come into play at this stage.

For example, I may want to grow my business by 30%, but give one night a week to the Blind Foundation. Technically, giving away one night will take me away from my vision, but part of my vision also is to remain 'human' and give back in some way to society.

As a sole trader it is also important to understand the difference between working IN the business rather than working ON. If we only ever work in, we will eventually burn out; we will also run out of customers because when we are working in, we may not be prospecting, or marketing or networking. A good ratio is 70% IN and 30% ON!

WHAT? What resources do you have and what resources

do you NOT have to help get you there? For example, I have a fully equipped office but I don't yet have a database of prospects. Or I have an office and a database, but don't have any office assistance to do the data inputting and invoicing. Remember you can't do everything yourself.

We often say 'I can't afford to pay anyone', when in fact we can't afford not to pay someone to do some of the admin work for us. Find a student or a solo mum who will be happy to work for a smaller fee than you might have to pay a professional secretarial service. Check out Upwork.com – a fabulous way to get work done and help people in third world countries earn an income.

The first meeting

STEP 1. It's important that you decide on your ground rules. This can be done by generally discussing the behaviours you DON'T want and then deciding the eight or ten behaviours you DO want. For example, we want people to arrive on time; to stick to their allotted time for speaking; to listen when other people are speaking).

These ground rules are not set in concrete. If after a few get togethers issues arise which some members are finding irritating, it is OK to have some time out to discuss the ground rules again.

A few key points here: focus on behaviours not

personalities (I'm having difficulty with people arriving late or I'm having difficulty when people set their goals for the month that they come back having done nothing, we are ALL busy people). When stating your concerns, use 'I' statements: '"I" have difficulty when people ...'. Offer some solutions: 'What would work better for me is ...')

STEP 2. Decide on the mechanics of the meetings. Where, when, how often, duration, format. With our group we had no formal leader; we met fortnightly for breakfast, the meeting lasted from 7 a.m. to 8.30. Our process was that each person spent a couple of minutes sharing our achievements of the past two weeks. We then shared any challenges we were having which gave members of the group an opportunity to offer ideas/suggestions or even to offer their time outside the meeting, to coach a member. We would end the meeting by setting our goals for the next two weeks.

STEP 3. Each person shares their Vision (where they want to be in five years).

STEP 4. Self-acknowledgement. It's important for each member of the group to acknowledge the areas they want the group to assist them (businesswise and personally). For example, 'I know that my time management isn't the best and I give the group full permission to prod me every now and again if it looks like I am slipping in this area.'

STEP 5. Every now and again set some time aside for a

debrief. Ask how the meetings are working for everyone; discuss what could be done to make it better.

Why mastermind groups make a difference

1. They are focussed. Each person states clearly what they want from the group with regard to growing their business and their character.

2. They create accountability. There is something about having said 'over the next two weeks I will ...'. One of our ground rules was that if a person didn't show up for two sessions, or twice in a row didn't complete their action points, they would be asked to leave. No-one EVER put themselves in that situation in our group!!

3. Mastermind groups create self-knowledge; they make us look in the mirror with particular regard to our purpose, results and our true motivation.

4. Like-minded people create synergy. Ideas will bounce around like lightening because of the personalities and entrepreneurial energy of the participants.

5. They are totally, and sometimes brutally honest. If a person starts playing 'games', they are very obvious in a small group and it's up to the group to gently and kindly assist that person to take a look at the results they are

achieving or not, and to take responsibility for their own part in these outcomes.

Creating your vision

To be filled in BEFORE a person comes to the first meeting.

Where would you aim if you knew you couldn't fail?

In five years I would like to have achieved:

....

....

....

....

That's important to me because:

....

....

....

....

How I will get there is:

....

....

....

....

The resources/skills/talents I currently have are:

....

....

....

....

The resource/skills/talents I will need are:

....

....

....

....

To be on track, in two years I would then have to be:

....

....

....

....

And in one year I would have to be:

....

....

....

....

In six months I would have to be:

....

....

....

....

Goal Planning Sheet

GOALS: (SMARTS = Specific, Measurable, Attainable, Realistic, Timeframe, **Stretch**). It's no use setting goals that help you stay in the same spot!

My 90 DAY GOALS are:

1 ....

....

2 ....

....

3 ....

....

4 ....

....

5 ....

....

60 DAYS:

1 ....

....

2 ....

....

3 ....

....

4 ....

....

5 ....

....

30 DAYS (which translates into an action plan):

1 ....

....

2 ....

....

3 ....

....

4 ....

....

5 ....

....

Further Reading

Did I Really Employ You? – Ann Andrews

Profitable Partnerships – Greg Nathan

The 'E' Myth – Michael Gerber

Your Life Your Legacy – Roger Hamilton

For a free basic profile go to: https://www.123test.com/

All of Ann's books plus her FREE e-books can be found on her website: www.annandrews.co.nz

About the author

Ann Andrews CSP is a seriously inspirational entrepreneur who spent 30+ years as an HR specialist encouraging organisations and individuals to learn, unlearn and relearn so they could face any change or challenge likely to hit their lives, careers or businesses.

Her early experience in the military exposed her to astounding leadership skills and an unusual way of working she still passes on because she firmly believes that if business understood the power of unleashing their people, they would be staggered at the results they could achieve.

A seasoned conference speaker, Ann is regularly invited back to challenge people with her infectious humour, real life stories and readily implemented, common sense tips. One organisation had her speak at their conference five years running!

Ann specializes as a conference 'opener' but can be effective as a break between technical topics or even as the after lunch presenter. She has presented at conferences around the world, including Hong Kong, Singapore, Belgium, Australia, Fiji and London.

A past National President of the National Speakers' Association of New Zealand, she was the recipient of The Spirit of Excellence Award in 2000 and again in 2009. This is the highest award in the New Zealand speaking profession. In 2015 she was inducted as a Life Member of NSANZ.

Ann has written six business books, co-authored a further eight and writes endless business e-books.

www.annandrews.co.nz

Other books by the author

Shift Your But (Self-published 1999)

Finding the Square Root of a Banana (Self-published 2000)

Did I Really Employ You? (Published by Reed Publishing (NZ), 2004)

My Dear Franchisees (2nd edition) (Published by Activity Press 2019)

Excellent Employment: Hiring the best people to help your business grow (Published by A & C Black, UK, 2007)

Mum's the Word by Vanessa Sunde, Kenina Court and Ann Andrews (Published by Phantom Publishing, 2007)

Lessons in Leadership: 50 Way to Avoid Falling into the 'Trump' Trap (Published by Moreau Publishing, 2017)

Leaders Behaving Badly: What happens when ordinary people show up, stand up and speak up (Published by Activity Press 2018)

E-books

Dealing with Resistance to Change (2005)

It's Just a Numbers Game: How to set up a training/ consulting business from scratch (2006)

Thousands of People Want to Do Business With You Can They Find You? (2008)

12 Steps to Running Great Meetings (2009)

How to Write an E-book in 5 days (2009)

Warning: Unsafe Acts Can Cause Major Headaches (2012)

Bullies at Work (2014) The 4 Stage Coaching Process (2015)

Fun and Games at Work (2016)

The 7 Tragic Ways Businesses Sabotage Their Own Success (2017)

Four Quadrant Leadership (2017

How to Deal With Poor Performance (2019)

How to Turn Whinging, Whining Groups, into High performing Teams (2019)